The Credit System

HOW TO PREVENT, CONTROL AND ELIMINATE CLASSROOM DISCIPLINE PROBLEMS

By ART KAPLAN

Published by Book Baby, Inc.

Printes in the United States of America

Library of Congress Cataloging-in-Publication Data

Kaplan, Art, 1941–

The Credit System. How to Prevent, Control, and Eliminate
Classroom Disciple Problems/Art Kaplan

ISBN 978-1-79230-087-5

TABLE OF CONTENTS

PREFACE

This book is about classroom discipline problems and the methods developed and refined to prevent and eliminate them from my classroom. The methods described, require no special materials other than a seating plan book or chart. The teacher who invests a few extra minutes a day, required to carry out the System, will be rewarded by discipline-free hours in his or her classroom.

Much of the material in this book was presented in a mini-course, given for guidance counselors, which concerned the controlling of discipline problems in the classroom. I was invited to attend this mini-course because of my work in this area. My ideas opened the eyes of these counselors; I gave them a "new" way to solve the age-old number one problem of the schools, controlling student behavior problems.

While every classroom situation is different, the basic ideas which I present can be instituted in any classroom. I hope that teachers, and all those concerned with controlling discipline in the schools, will familiarize themselves with the material in this book in order to use these methods as a tool to increase the productivity and happiness of both teacher and student.

INTRODUCTION

Is there any doubt that classroom discipline problems are the number one problem in today's schools? If we could eliminate these problems, everyone would be happier. The teachers, because they would be able to teach, the parents because their children would be learning, and the students themselves, because they would get the feeling that coming to school was really worth the time and effort they put into it.

So let's get rid of these problems, RIGHT NOW! I am a ten-year veteran of the New York City Public School System, and in those years I made a discovery which helped me prevent, control and eliminate classroom behavior problems. By reading this book you will learn this easy method and learn how to put it into effect immediately. In a matter of minutes your classroom will change from a place where students may resent coming, to a place where students will want to come and learn. It's fast, easy, requires only a seating plan book or seating plan chart and a little extra time to make the plan work.

So get ready, get set, and go get a pencil to take notes as you read. I'm giving you over ten years' worth of in-class expertise on classroom discipline in a few pages. I guarantee that the ideas in this book will change your ideas about classroom discipline forever. Study this book carefully and put it into action as soon as possible. Your students will thank you for it.

SECTION 1

THE FIRST DAY: SETTING UP THE SYSTEM

CHAPTER I: THE ART OF POSITIVE THINKING

While many bad things can be happening in a classroom, it is far more likely that there are many more good things going on. What kind of good things? When a student pays attention to a lesson, takes notes, participates in a class discussion, does his homework, is helpful in some way to the teacher (monitorial), or his fellow students, all of these types of things are **"observable positive behavior."** This positive behavior many not be noticed as much by teachers because it is "expected" but it is there and should be noticed just as much or even more so than negative behavior. Unfortunately, trouble-makers are usually given the attention they want, while the students who are doing a good job may be virtually ignored.

It was my idea that if somehow I could **reward** this observable positive behavior, I could encourage its continuance and limit the misdeeds that begin to appear and develop in the classroom like weeds in a garden.

The idea of giving rewards for positive behavior in the classroom is not a new one; in fact, it goes back almost 200 years. Diane Ravitch, the famed educational historian, wrote in the *New York Times* that in "New York's public school in the 1830's good children were rewarded with praise, merit badges, and tickets which could be saved and exchanged for toys." (*New York Times*, Sec. IV, Page 8, 7/7/74) Unfortunately, Ms. Ravitch doesn't tell us, in this article, how successful or prevalent these programs actually were. Neither does she explain how these ideas were implemented in the classroom.

Many teachers, administrators and parents may feel that rewarding "expected good behavior" is wrong. I feel that rewards, awards and prizes are part of our society. Winning the Nobel Prize, the Pulitzer Prize or an Academy Award are examples of types of rewards for outstanding achievement. In everyday life, a salary check can be considered a reward earned for doing a good job.

If adults receive rewards, why not have a similar attitude for work done in the classroom? Of course, teachers may feel that the knowledge gained by the students in learning the subject matter is the reward, eventually leading to good grades, admission to college and a good job.

This may be true up to a point. Unfortunately, these long term rewards may not be satisfying to many students, especially since many of these future rewards will never come.

Traditional Positive Classroom Awards

I am sure many of you have tried some type of positive motivation at one time or another. A word of praise for some good piece of work is always appropriate. Rewarding good students with monitorial jobs, hanging good written work on the class bulletin boards are examples of good positive techniques. Giving out certificates for good grades, attendance and punctuality are traditional in many schools.

The problem with these traditional techniques is they are not lasting. When an academically borderline student flunks an exam, what then will his paper hanging on the bulletin board be worth? What about the effort made by that student during a class discussion?

In this book, I will show you how you can make observable positive behavior into something of real "value" to all students. I will discuss positive techniques that are not random but are part of a system that the teacher sets up and incorporates as part of his or her every day class. I hope you will read the following chapters carefully, understand the ideas and use them in your classroom. If you do, I know you will be surprised by the **POWER** of the system to prevent, control and eliminate classroom behavior problems.

CHAPTER II: YOU'RE ON YOUR WAY: THE BEGINNING

The day you begin, you will be amazed at the immediate positive reaction of the class, so be prepared!

On the first day of class (if it is the beginning of the school year), organize the student seating arrangements anyway you wish (size place I find is best). I suggest you use a seating plan book or chart. The most useful type of books are those that come with cards, that fit in slots (on the pages) which correspond to the seats in the class. (The Delaney and Arco Companies put out such a book.) This seating plan book will be most helpful in carrying out the System described in this book.

After the class is seated, have them fill out the seating plan cards and place the cards in the appropriate slots. **You are now ready to speak the "magic words" to your class that will set in motion the powerful system of discipline control that will enable you to teach without the behavior problems that disrupt many of today's classrooms.**

Tell the class that, in the time they spend in your classroom, **you are going to look for good and/or helpful things that they are doing.** These things can be oral, written or monitorial in nature, as long as it is something that is helpful to the student himself, the teacher, another student, the class as a whole, or even the school. **When one of these positive things is done by a student, that student will receive a mark on his**

card (the seating plan card). The mark resembles the number "1" and represents "one good thing the student has done." The name that I have given to these marks is **CREDITS.** Therefore, the name of the system described in this book will be referred to as **THE CREDIT SYSTEM.**

I now continue to explain to the class that as these credits accumulate, the students will be able to **"trade in or buy" various rewards** which the students might like. (These rewards will be discussed later). Credits are like money in the bank, they have to be **earned** by the student and then afterwards they can be **used or saved** as the student desires.

You will find the reaction of the class to be very positive. I have had classes come into my room totally unmotivated but raring to go to work after the Credit System is explained.

On the first day, there is one other very important thing to speak to the class about concerning the Credit System, that being, the relationship between the student's accumulated credits and his **conduct mark.** Most schools require the student to receive a conduct or attitude mark on the report card, as well as a mark for the subject matter. **Tell the students that if they have a certain number of credits at the end of each marking period, they will receive the highest conduct mark (usually "A" or "E").** Therefore, at the end of each marking period, the number of credits required for an "A" in conduct is crossed off the student's card. Any credits over that number will remain on the card and be carried over to the next marking period. I have found anywhere between 25 to 50 credits should be set, by the teacher, to meet this "requirement."

For example, let us say you decide that each student must have 50 credits to get an "A" in conduct. Say at the end of the marking period, a student has accumulated 60 credits. 50 credits are crossed off the student's card and he begins the next marking period with 10 credits. The removal of credits to "pay" for an "A" in conduct I call the **CONDUCT TAX.**

Another rule to tell the class is that although credits are usable, they cannot be used until the amount of credits needed to pay the Conduct Tax is reached, and only those credits over that number can be "spent." For example, a student has accumulated 95 credits before the end of a marking period (say the Conduct Tax is 50 credits), he can only use 45 credits for other things, 50 credits must be saved to be used to pay the Conduct Tax. If he has under 50 credits he would not be allowed to use any of them.

What if a student doesn't reach the amount needed for an "A"? If the student's behavior is good he can still get an "A" but, of course, he will not be able to spend his credits on anything else. For example, let us assume you make 50 credits the Conduct Tax, if the student has 40 credits at the end of the marking period, all his credits are crossed out and he starts the next marking period with no credits.

What if a student has the 50 credits for an "A" but his conduct doesn't really deserve it? In following chapters, I will tell you about a technique to handle this situation.

To summarize:

1. **Credits represent good work by a student.**
2. **Good work may be written, oral or monitorial.**
3. **Students may save up their credits or use them if they so choose. (The students control their credits)**
4. **A predetermined number of credits must be accumulated during a marking period to pay for the Conduct Tax. These credits cannot be spent.**
5. **Credits accumulated over the Conduct Tax requirement may be spent at any time.**
6. **At the end of a marking period, not before, the amount of credits needed to pay the Conduct Tax is removed and the student receives an "A." Any extra credits are carried over to the next marking period.**
7. **If a student doesn't have enough credits to meet the Conduct Tax Requirement he may still receive an "A" if his conduct warrants it, but he starts the next marking period with zero credits.**

You are now on your way to controlling student behavior in your classroom. By instituting the Credit System, you have in effect told the students that positive acts will not only be noticed by you, but will be permanently recorded. The good work they do during your classes will NOT be forgotten. Credits enable the teacher to quantify the qualitative nature of "good work." **In**

addition, you have given each student an immediate reason to earn credits: a good grade in conduct.

Even the most troublesome student will rightly think he has a chance to reach this goal. Conduct is judged on a predetermined impersonal number and not on the likes or dislikes of the teacher. In many of my classes, I've had students who are considered troublemakers in other classes and I didn't even know it.

After this discussion, the students will have many questions. One of the most common is "What if I don't get enough credits to get an "A"? Simply tell the student that, you the teacher, will then have to be the judge if the student deserves an "A" or not, just like in any other class. Advise them "not to worry at this time."

Questions about other uses for credits will probably be asked. The following chapters in this book will give you the answers to most of these questions.

CHAPTER III: THE CREDIT SYSTEM - THE MECHANICS

Teachers who first try the Credit System may find that entering credits on students' seating plan cards, or seating charts, a bit of a psychological problem. They may feel that they cannot continually enter credit throughout a class period, while at the same time carrying out a meaningful lesson. There are ways of getting around this "problem," which will be discussed in this chapter, but first I would like to ask the reader, **How much do behavior problems contribute to a lesson?** The reduction of discipline problems and poor work habits and the increase of positive behavior, by the students, is well worth the small amount of extra minutes needed to make the System work. The fact is that once you begin the System you will want it to work! **AND IT WILL!**

Much of the credit earned by the students will be on written work. Since written work can be collected, credits can be entered by the teacher after class. This presents no more difficulty than marking any other set of papers. I will explore these ideas in the following chapters.

Entering credits in the classroom requires that the seating plan book or chart always be out and available to the teacher. This would probably be true in any case since at the beginning of the term the teacher is getting to know the names of the students in his or her class. If the teacher moves around the room, the book may be carried but this is not always necessary.

During class discussion, the teacher may feel that entering credits can interfere with the continuous flow of ideas. In "less-motivated" classes, the constant reinforcement of *seeing* the teacher entering credits for answers and questions is just the thing that will keep everything going. In more "self-motivated" classes, credit may be given after the discussion has ended, during a "quiet" time.

By entering credits, the teacher will find a greater number of students will participate in the discussion. Many "behavior" problem children will be getting an immediate and lasting reward (a credit) when they participate and therefore will be more likely to pay attention for further rewards.

As for the teacher, when he or she sees the enthusiasm generated by awarding credits during discussion, the teacher will be self-motivated to train himself or herself to give credit during these times.

Since the seating plan card plays such a key role in the System, I would like to discuss the way the card should be used. Seating plan charts can be used as well, but they are less flexible. If you have to use a seating plan chart, it should be one which has plenty of room in the space provided to include the information I am presenting in this section of the chapter. You can always make up your own seating plan chart card.

When I first began using the Credit System, I marked a small "plus" on the card for each positive act of a student. However, this turned out to be too cumbersome.

I then hit upon the idea of using a small number "one" instead of a plus. Then the idea came to me that certain positive acts could be worth "more" than one credit. For example, if some positive act was worth two credits I could write a small "2." This took up very little space on the card, whereas before I would have had to write two· "plusses," now I only had to write a "2."

As the term goes on, credits continue to accumulate on the students' cards. The card becomes an easy way to see which students are contributing and which are not. The teacher may make an effort to look for the "quieter" students so as to add to their number of credits.

From time to time, you will have to count up the number of credits a student has accumulated. When you count up all the little ones, twos, etc. and get a total count, write that number on the card and circle it. Be sure to cross out all the small credit numbers so they cannot be counted a second time. For example, if the total number of credits on the card add up to 35 credits, cross out all the 1's, 2's, etc. and write 35 with a circle around it (35). This indicates 35 credits and not a 3 and a 5, which would only be eight credits.

Credit Counting is one of those extra things you will have to do from time to time. This will be a small price to pay for the many advantages gained from using the Credit System. Credit Counting will be discussed more fully later on in the book.

Remember, the above are merely suggestions based on my years of experience using the System. No matter how you write credits, or if you call them “plusses” or “points” the idea is the same: **Keep a physical record of the students’ positive behavior.**

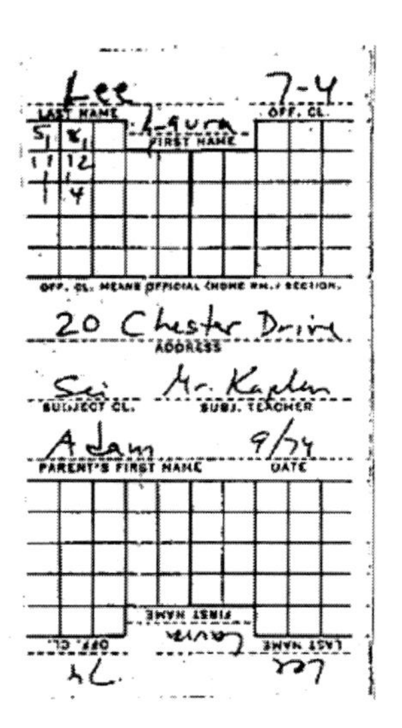
Lee 7-4
LAST NAME Laura OFF. CL.
FIRST NAME
OFF. CL. MEANS OFFICIAL (HOME RM.) SECTION.
20 Chester Drive
ADDRESS
Sci Mr. Kaplan
SUBJECT CL. SUBJ. TEACHER
Adam
PARENT’S FIRST NAME DATE

To the left is a sample of a seating plan card. The numbers are credits earned by the student. When they are “used” they are crossed off the card. In the sample card, the student has a total of 27 credits

SECTION 2

WHY STUDENTS WANT CREDITS: THE REWARDS

CHAPTER IV:
REWARDS FOR GOOD BEHAVIOR

The credit is the basis of the Credit System. It is not only an **immediate** reward for some positive act by the student, but also has a **quantitative value.** The amount of the students' positive behavior is recorded by the teacher, just as marks are recorded for tests, quizzes, reports, etc. As the school year goes on, the number of credits the student earns will continue to grow.

You may find that students will try to keep track of the number of credits they have earned. Often, they may ask you how many credits they have earned. Here is how to tell them. On some regular basis collect a sheet of paper from each student. The sheet should have written on it the student's name and class. After class, or at home, spend a few minutes counting up the credits for each child. Write the credits on his sheet. The next day, hand the sheets directly back to each student, do not use monitors. You will see the excitement of the class when they get these sheets back, especially when this is done the first time. This procedure I call **Credit Counting.** The small amount of time this process takes is well worth the good behavior the Credit System establishes in your class.

Another way to inform students of the amount of credits they have on their cards (I call this a **Credit Balance**) is to write the number on some collected piece of written work such as a test or homework. Therefore, the student gets back his test and a credit balance as well.

If a student is "dying" to know his credit balance – this is usually before the student is going to use the credits for some reward – he can do this by a special count. The **<u>Special Count</u>** enables the student to know his credit balance at any time, but the student must **PAY** one credit (1+). (Incidentally, I use a small plus sign as the symbol for a credit.) To do this he just hands in a headed sheet of paper and writes on it "special count." I make it a policy that all rewards offered by the Credit System, **must be requested for in writing**. The student may request these rewards using his own sheet of paper or a form which you can make up which I call a request sheet. So here is a simple use the student has for his credits. Of course, if the student waits, he can find out his credit balance for **FREE**.

* * * * *

Previously, I wrote that credits could be used by students for some other rewards. In this part of the chapter I would like to suggest some possible rewards that credits could be traded in for. You, the teacher, can use these suggestions in your classroom or add any others you can think of that would be appropriate for your class and grade level. **<u>The more uses for credits the more valuable they become</u>**.

The rewards I have used are rewards based on conduct, work, and rewards within the Credit System.

THE CREDIT ITSELF- The credit itself is a sense of accomplishment for a student. The more the students accumulate, the better they feel. Also, a large number of credits will give students a sense of security. They know they have the credits to use if they really need them. **I have found that since the accumulation of credits is the greatest reward of the Credit System, you will never be overwhelmed by requests for rewards**.

THE CONDUCT MARK - (35+ - 50+) Note: after each reward I will give you a suggested value. (The value is the amount of credits that are removed from a student's credit balance to receive a reward.) I have already discussed the conduct mark in a previous chapter. I should note that it is different than most of the other rewards I will write about, in that it is **required** to be "paid" for, at the end of each marking period.

All the following rewards are similar in that they are **voluntary**, that is, the student **must request** them. The rewards and their values should be made known to the class in some manner (on a bulletin board). Requests should be **handed in** on a piece of paper, never orally. After a reward has been given, remember to remove the credits needed to pay for the reward from the student's card. Remember, only the credits above those needed to pay the conduct tax may be used for these rewards. The following rewards are based on good student classroom behavior:

1 - **THE GOOD LETTER** - (20+)
This is a personal letter written by the teacher to the child's parents or anyone else the child wants it sent to. (This letter often makes a nice birthday present for a parent or grandparent), If possible, it should be written

on school stationery. The letter can praise the behavior and/or the child's work, but <u>it must be the truth.</u>
If the child wants this reward (or any reward) but the child's behavior or work has not been good enough, you should use the technique that I call **PROBATION**. Probation is the delaying of a reward for a specific time period during which the student makes an attempt to improve on his behavior or work. Probation uses "immediacy of a reward" as a reward in itself. For example, a child wants a reward but he has been "acting up," tell him that you will put him on "probation" for one week. If he improves he may resubmit his request.

2 - **GOOD TELEPHONE CALL** - (20+)
This reward is similar to the good letter but there is more immediacy and direct vocal contact. This reward is useful if the parents do not read English that well. The student should indicate on his request sheet if there is a preference as to which parent to speak to and the best time to call.

3 - **LETTER OF COMMENDATION** - (15+)
This is a form letter to someone in the school to let that person know about some positive thing that student has done in your class. This letter may be especially useful for those students who have been in trouble, have had run-ins with school authorities, or have been involved with deans and guidance counselors. Such a letter might be the first step in turning a troublemaker around.

Through the Credit System I have been able to motivate the students to continue good behavior by showing them that good behavior pays. Not only by earning A's on their report cards or by letting others know of their effort, but also that good behavior can translate into good work as well. I will discuss the rewards based on good work in the next chapter.

CHAPTER V:
CREDITS AND STUDENTS' GRADES

1 - **THE CREDIT** - (1+)
This reward is given for written, oral and monitorial work. How credits are earned will be discussed in following chapters.

2 - **RAISING OF TEST MARKS** - (5+ for 1 pt. raised on a major exam)
In my classes, a student may raise a test mark up to 99%. (100% cannot be achieved by using credits) In order to do this, the student **must hand back his test paper** with a request sheet, telling me how many points should **be added to the test mark. (This technique forces students to save their tests and not toss them into the trash can.)** I take the request sheet and, after class, change the test grade (on the paper and my marking book), cross out the correct number of credits (5+ for each point) and hand the test back to the student the next day. The same test may be raised as many times as the student wishes.

By enabling students the right to raise their test scores, I have enabled them to transfer the observable positive behavior, they exhibit during class, into "real" meaning, the increase of their work marks.

3 - **ELIMINATION OF TEST MARKS** - (50+ per major test)
Sometimes a student will get a very low mark on a major test which would take too many credits to raise it to

a respectful grade. For 50+ I permit students to eliminate this test grade. My conditions are:

1. The student must hand in the test and

2. Only one exam may be eliminated for each marking period.

For example, if it is the 3rd marking period, any three exams may be eliminated no matter in which marking period they were given. The teacher should schedule at least three or four major exams (tests worth 100%) during each marking period. And

3. The student must have taken a certain minimum number of tests before a grade can be eliminated. The formula I use is: Number of major exams minus the current marking period. For example: if the class has been given eight tests and it is the 3rd marking period, the minimum number of tests required, for each student is five. Therefore, if a student has taken seven tests, he may eliminate two test marks.

4 - **ELIMINATION OF OTHER PIECES OF MARKED WRITTEN WORK** – (the value depends on the work itself)

A- Quizzes - Marks on short quizzes are not permitted to be changed. They may be eliminated for a charge of 5+ per question. For example, a bad mark, on a five question quiz, may be eliminated for 25+.

B - Homework - If a homework assignment is to be collected and marked but a student doesn't hand it in, then credit may be deducted from his card so he doesn't get a "zero" grade. The amount of credit removed depends on the assignment (I usually make it 3+ to 5+ per question, depending on the difficulty of the question). Strictly speaking, this is NOT A REWARD since I do not make this "voluntary." In other words, if a student can afford to pay for not doing homework, HE MUST. Of course, you can let him make up the homework, give him back his credits but assess a late charge (5+ to 10+ depending on the homework.)

C - Reports - Major and minor report marks can be eliminated in the same manner as homework. You might make a major report have a value of 50+ or more. If it is not done, those credits are removed from a student's card. Always give students a chance to hand in reports after the assignment date, but set up some late charge; for example: 5+ for each day handed in late. You may even permit students to be excused from doing reports upon payment of credits. But as with the tests, there should be a minimum number of major reports required for the term. I have students write three major reports; they may eliminate only one by using their credits.

Raising of test marks and elimination of bad marks on quizzes and written work is one of the many advantages of using the Credit System. Students can do things in your class they could not do in others. They can help raise their work grades by raising test marks and eliminating poor marks on other forms of written work by using their credits. You will find that written work will be done, and usually on time, simply because the students do not want to lose credits.

Don't worry that students will eliminate so many marks that you won't have enough grades to mark them. First of all, they can use credits only above the number required to pay the conduct tax and secondly, no matter how many credits a student has, he will never have enough to do everything he wants. **The fact is, most students will save their credits and not use them except on rare occasions. You will never be overwhelmed by student requests.**

Some of you may have some doubts about the "ethics" of changing of test marks and elimination of test scores. I have found this to be one of the most powerful rewards I can offer. It is a way to translate the good work performed by a student during the everyday work of the class, into a quantitative value to use for his report card mark.

CHAPTER VI: UNIQUE CREDIT SYSTEM REWARDS

In this chapter, I will discuss several rewards that were invented to help the student within the classroom where the Credit System is used.

1 - THE SPECIAL COUNT - (1+)
This reward was written about in Chapter IV. If a student wants to know his or her credit balance (the amount of credits on his card) the student can request that you count his credits. The request should be in writing. After class, you count the credits, remove 1+ from the card, and write the amount down on the request sheet. The next time the class meets, hand back the request sheet with this credit balance.

2 - THE INSTANT REPORT CARD - (Suggested Value = 5+)
If a student would like to know what his grade would be if he was going to get his report card that day, he can find out by using this reward. After the request has been made, figure out the student's grade by totaling up all the marks. Hand the mark back to the student the next day. Remember to cross out 5+ for the reward.

3 - THE CREDIT BOND - (40+)
This reward takes advantage of the fact that accumulation of credits is a reward in and of itself. When a student requests a Credit Bond (see sample) I make out a certificate. Besides the student's name and my signature there is a redemption date. In my classes, the date I've used is 15 school days after issuing the Bond. For this

reward I deduct 40+ from a student's card and in turn write a small "B" on it. At the end of the time period, the student returns the Bond, I cross out the "B" and give the student 50+.

If a student has a Bond "out" but he needs credit for some other reward, he can hand back the Bond and his 40+ are returned. If a student loses the certificate, a new one is issued with a new redeemable date.

The Credit Bond is designed for students who have plenty of credits so the temporary loss of 40+ will not matter. The ability to earn credit through an "investment" is a lesson in everyday life. This reward has proved to be one of the most popular.

4 - **PRIVILEGE REWARDS** - (value varies)
These rewards give the student the right to do things in your class which he might not ordinarily be allowed to do, as long as it is not disruptive to the class as a whole. Such things as chewing gum, doing homework in class,

ANY SCHOOL USA

Credit Bond

50+

Name: ______________________________

Due Date: ____________________________

free time (in elementary grades), are examples of possible rewards.

Remember, just the fact that these things are available to the students make credits more valuable, but this does not mean that any of these things will be requested, since students will usually wish to accumulate credits rather than spend them.

In summary, the rewards of the Credit System are designed to help the student in areas of conduct, grades and other things within the class. All rewards must be requested in writing; remember to cross out the correct amount of credits after giving the student the requested reward.

Keep in mind, the majority of students will feel the greatest reward is the number of credits they have on their cards. You may even have to convince the students that they should spend their credits on the available rewards, including raising test marks.

Now you may ask, "What about all those credits at the end of the school year?" I tell my classes that all unused credits will be used to raising their grades on the Final Exam at the rate of 10+ per point since the Final is worth double in the average. If there are still credits remaining, I will use them up on regular tests (5+ per point).

*****

In the next section I will discuss how credits are actually earned in the classroom. There should be no doubt in your mind that students will want credits. Why? Because credits have real value for the student, whether the student wants credits to use to help him or wants them just to see how many he can earn. It is up to the teacher to provide the opportunities during the class so that credits can be earned.

Once again I want to stress that although there seems to be a lot of bookkeeping involved in giving these rewards there really is not. Very few students will ever ask for any of these rewards at any one time. Until the Credit System is started in your classroom, you may not believe me but it is true. **Remember, the greatest reward of all to the students is the ACCUMULATION of credits, not their use.**

SECTION 3

PUTTING CREDITS INTO ACTION!

THE EARNING OF CREDITS

CHAPTER VII:
ORAL CREDIT OPPORTUNITIES

In most classes, oral work is easily forgotten in the grading of the student; most marks depending on written work such as tests, quizzes, reports, work sheets, etc. The Credit System enables the student to transfer good oral work, in class, into a permanent record: THE CREDIT.

1 - **CLASS DISCUSSION** - (1+ per answer or question)

If a student gives an answer, asks a good question or comes up with an insight into the lesson, this is positive observable behavior. In less motivated classes ("slow"), it is preferable to reinforce this behavior by giving credit as much as possible. In more motivated classes, this may not be necessary. Instead, at the end of the period, you can give credit to those students who actively participated.

In class discussion, the teacher should require that students first **raise their hands** and be called on. If a student calls out an answer, no credit should be given, even if the answer is correct. This technique I call **denying credit.** Denying credit will easily eliminate the poor work habit of "calling out." For example: I might ask the class "What science studies about living things?" A student shouts out "Biology." I tell him that since he did not follow the rules of class discussion I cannot give him credit. I then ask the question to the class. This time everyone will raise his hand, you can bet on that. If you want to be really tough, you can tell the class that if someone **shouts out** the wrong answer they will lose one credit. (If they answer a question incorrectly but they raised their hand, they do not lose any credits.)

Another thing students may do is ask you if they received credit for an answer. The first time this happens, tell them that "if any student asks me if they earned a credit for an answer, they will not get credit." Denying credit in this situation will prevent students from continually asking this question.

So you see, not only does the Credit System reward class discussion, but it is also a powerful tool in establishing class routines such as "how to ask and answer questions in a proper manner."

2 - **ORAL QUIZZES** - (1+ per correct answer)
At the beginning of a period, I spend about five minutes asking the class questions dealing with any topic they are studying. Questions may be based on classwork, homework, reports, the test, etc. Credit is given for correct answers that are answered in a proper manner. Oral quizzes may also be given at the end of the period as well, questions being based on the lesson. The oral quiz may be open or closed book.

Oral quizzes serve as a good way to get the class settled down and into a learning mood at the beginning of a class, as well as a good review and, of course, as a way to earn some credits.

3 - **READING** - (1+ per reading)
Reading may be from texts, notebooks, filmstrips, reports, etc. Once again, deny credit to any student who intentionally doesn't read properly, if you judge he is trying to be a "wise guy." Also, you might ask the class

questions about the reading, giving credit to correct answers.

4 - **STUDENT PARTICIPATION** - (1+ per)
Sometimes a teacher may need a student to help in some demonstration. I teach science, and very frequently it is necessary to have one or more students help out with a science experiment. This lends itself easily to giving out credit.

* * * * *

Positive oral work is easily translated to a mark by use of credits. It also makes it easy to establish classroom rules of participation. One thing I will tell you is that you must be very <u>consistent</u> so that no student feels that he didn't get a credit when he should have. If you're going to change rules on how credits are going to be earned, it should be announced at the beginning, and not during, a class.

CHAPTER VIII:
WRITTEN CREDIT OPPORTUNITIES

Written work provides numerous opportunities for students to earn credits. In this chapter, I will discuss these different types of written work. Some types of written work can be combined with oral and monitorial opportunities to earn credit. At the same time, I will show you how the Credit System can be used to correct student poor work habits usually associated with written work .

Written work is usually graded with a numerical or alphabetical mark. Using the Credit System, you should continue to give these types of marks but, in addition, you can supplement the mark by giving credits as well. For example, credits can be added to reports for neatness, for being handed in on time, etc. The report's content would still be marked with the numerical or alphabetical grade. In Chapter V, I discussed students' use of credits to "pay" for being excused from doing reports.

Another option the teacher has is to mark a piece of written work in credits only. Here is an example of a type of written work that would be almost impossible to give a meaningful grade to without the Credit System. I might tell the students to make a list of as many objects they find in the room. I also tell them that for every five objects, they write down, they will receive 1+. In order to receive credits, each object on the list must be numbered. I usually give them a limited amount of time they can work, at the end of which their papers are collected. For example: a student writes down 37 objects, his "mark" is 7+ for his paper. (I call this type of written work "unlimited" since there is no limit to the amount of credits a student may earn). I think you can imagine the enthusiasm of the students participating in this activity; everyone will earn some credits and there are no falling marks.

To summarize, the Credit System provides a way of marking almost any kind of work that goes on in the classroom. Since students want, and in many cases need, credits they will do things that they might ordinarily not do without a great deal of coaxing. The teacher will find that he or she will be able to direct many class activities without any trouble.

In the following section, I am going to list some specific written work activities and how I would use the Credit System to have the students carry them out. After each credit opportunity listed, I will write an **"O"** if an oral opportunity and/or an **"M"** if a monitorial opportunity can be used with the written opportunity.

* * * * *

1 - **CLASSNOTES** -
On occasion, near the end of a class, I will collect class notes from that day's lesson, either from the entire class or just three or four students. After school, I take the papers and figure out the "value" of the notes. For example: the day's notes consist of two diagrams, three definitions and a chart. I might make each diagram worth 2+, the definitions worth 1+ each and the chart worth 3+. The total value of notes would be 10+ if all the parts were written correctly and clearly.

This technique of figuring the value of student written work is done over and over again. Simply figure out the important points of your lesson, give some value to them and add up the points and/or credits to give the total work a value.

As far as note taking goes, you might or might not announce to the class your intentions of collecting notes at the end of the period. However, the collecting of notes will be seen as a reward by the students since it gives them a chance to earn credits. I would mark on the students' cards an "N" each time I collect that student's notes so as to remember who and who has not had their notes collected. By the way, if the notes collected are incomplete, the student should get no credit, but give him a day to hand in the corrected notes. However, he is not entitled to full credit (I usually give half the credits that the student would been entitled to if the notes had been complete in the first place).

Another technique I use is to call up two or three students for a quick look at their notes. If they seem in order they will get 2+. During the lesson you might take note of students who do not seem to be paying attention. Call these students up at the end of the class for a note check. If the notes are incomplete have the students do it over to be handed in the next day.

2 - **FILMSTRIPS** - (O and M)

Using filmstrips is a useful audio-visual aid. They permit the student to see pictures on the subject matter, read orally and take notes. The Credit System will enable the teacher to carry out a successful filmstrip lesson with plenty of credit opportunities for the students.

Here is an outline of how you might conduct a film-strip lesson with the help of credits:

A- Select monitors for shades, screen and lights (Give 2+ for doing the job properly. If job is not done well then no credits are given.)

B- Select a monitor to run the projector. The job done properly is worth 5+. (Naturally, lots of volunteers for this job, so mark a "P" on card to show that student was a projectionist).

C- Have students read captions. Give 1+ for each correct reading; deny credit to students who do not read properly.

D- Students are to have a piece of paper on their desks at beginning of filmstrip. Students should head their papers with their name, class and film title. Have students copy down captions or facts from the filmstrip. They should number each fact they write down. Announce that their papers will be collected and marked at the rate of 1+ for every five facts.

E- After filmstrip, conduct an oral quiz based on the filmstrip (1+ for each correct answer).

F- Collect papers at end of class. Mark at the pre-announced rate and hand back the next day.

3 - **MOVIES and VIDEO TAPES** (O and M)

A- "Hire" monitors to set up room. (See filmstrips)

B- Have students take out a sheet of paper. Have them put their name, class and title of film/tape on the paper.

C- Tell them that on the paper they must write at least five facts from the film or tape.

D- At end of film or tape, conduct an oral quiz by calling on students to make up a question about a fact in the film (give 1+). Call on students to answer the questions (1+ for correct answer).

E- Collect papers and give credit mark (5+)

F- Return papers the next day.

4 - **HOMEWORK** - Homework may be checked from time to time. If homework is based on questions asked in a textbook or work book, they should be marked with a numerical or alphabetical grade. Credits can be used to reward neatness of work (1+) and handing it in on time (1+).

You may assign other types of homework that could be marked only by credits. For example: "Make a list of chemicals and their uses that are found in your home." They should number each chemical and use. Mark at the rate of 1+ per five chemicals and uses. This is another example of unlimited written work. As before, credits can be given for neatness and being on time.

5 - **MAJOR REPORTS** - I assign three major reports during the school year. These reports are given a maximum numerical value of 100%. They are equivalent in value to major exams. Credits can be used to reward neatness and handing them in on time. A student may be excused from one of the reports for 50+, if he has done at least two reports during the term. Students may write all three reports and decide to eliminate the report

with the lowest grade. On the date the reports are due, I run a lesson as follows:

A- All students take out a blank sheet of paper. They write their name and class on it.

B- Select a volunteer to read his report (3+).

C- Volunteer puts name of report on chalk board.

D- Class copies name of report and volunteer.

E- During reading, class copies down five facts from the report. (1+ per five facts)

F- At end of reading, I conduct a short oral quiz based on the report, with students making up questions (1+). You call on students for answers (1+)

G- Repeat B-F for rest of period.

H- Collect fact sheets and give credit mark later. Return fact sheets the next day.

I- Collect major reports.

6 - **SHORT WRITTEN QUIZZES** -
These quizzes are given at the beginning of a period in place of oral quizzes. After papers are given out, the students write their headings. I read a question and the students write the answers, they do not write the question. After one or two minutes I read another question, and so on. These quizzes may consist of up to five questions. The quiz is given a numerical grade. The final question is an "unlimited" type question marked with credits. For example: name as many _____ as you can. (1+ for every five things named.)

Using this type of question at the end of a test or quiz keeps students working right to the time you call an end to the quiz. Remember that poor grades on these short written quizzes may be eliminated by students if they so wish.

7 - **EXTRA CREDIT REPORTS** - (10+ – 20+)
I give my students opportunities to earn credit by letting them write extra credit reports. I make the following rules:

A- Student must have topic okayed by me.

B- Only one extra credit report allowed per marking period.

C- Reports will be marked by credits only, 20+ maximum.

8 - **WORK SHEETS** -
In science, certain periods are devoted to lab work in which work sheets are used by the students. These work sheets contain questions which are marked with a numerical grade. Usually, students work together in groups of three or four, and these groups are judged and given credits based on how they work during this period. Since students want to earn credits, as well as get a good mark, there is strong peer pressure not to fool around during these times. At the end of the period, work sheets are handed in. After class, you mark them and give credit marks for neatness (1+) and good working skills (5+). During these periods, hire monitors for handing out and collecting equipment.

9 - **RESEARCH LESSONS** -

In these lessons, students use books to answer questions. The questions are printed on a sheet. Usually, I have the students write directly on this sheet. Questions are marked numerically except for some that I might mark with credits (making lists). A neatness credit mark 1+ or 2+ is also given. In effect, the research lesson is an open book test which I use mainly with my less motivated classes.

* * * * *

In this chapter, I have given you examples of types of written work that lend themselves to the Credit System. I am sure most of you use many of these same things in your classes. If you use activities in your classes that are not described in this chapter, try to think of how you may incorporate the Credit System to become part of them.

In the next chapter I will show you how the Credit System is used with one of the most important types of written work, the Major Exam.

CHAPTER IX-
CREDITS AND THE MAJOR EXAM

Like it or not, the test remains the main way of determining students' grades, at least on the secondary level. In my classes, I usually give three full-period major exams in a marking period. In addition, I give a midterm and final exam. All these tests are marked using number grades, which can be raised or eliminated by the students using their credits.

In previous chapters, I have written about the Credit System's ability to encourage students to write neatly, such as in reports. Also, credits may be earned in tests for neatness, and when unlimited-types of questions or extra-credit questions are included.

In my classes, the major exam is preceded the day before by a test preview, followed the next day by the test itself. When the test is marked, it is returned after a review of the exam. In each case, the Credit System is in use to encourage class participation.

THE TEST PREVIEW

Previews can simply be the asking of questions followed by answers as in the oral quizzes. However, in my classes, the preview is in the form of games, which work very nicely with the Credit System. The game may be in the form of a class tic-tac-toe game, an individual crossword or word search sheet which I prepare in advance.

TIC-TAC-TOE

This game is run as follows:

1 - Have class take out blank sheets of paper and have them put their names and classes on it.

2 - Tell them that they are to write as many questions as they can about the topic the test will be on. They must number each question but they don't have to answer the question. They may use their notebook s as sources of questions.

3 - While they are writing, draw a tic-tac-toe on the board with the squares numbered from 1 to 9.

4 - Collect papers after five minutes.

5 - Divide class into two teams, the X's and the O's.

6 - Read one of the questions written by a student and ask the question.

7 - Select the first hand raised, if the student answers correctly, he chooses any box of the tic-tac-toe to put his X or O. The student comes up to the chalk board to do this and receives 1+ for his correct answer.

8 - I read another question, only members of the other team may answer and if correct he gets 1+ and puts his X or O on the board. A student may answer only once during a game.

9 - If an answer is incorrect, I ask a student volunteer on the other team for the answer. He gets 1+ for a correct answer, but does not put a X or O on the board.

10 - After a wrong answer, the team that missed goes again with a new question. This goes on until one of the teams win or there is a tie.

11 - Scoring: For each game won, every member of the winning team gets 2+, if a tie, everyone in class gets 1+ (this is true even if they haven't answered a question).

12 - Penalties: If an answer is called out, the team of that student loses their turn and the other team goes. I usually read the same question.

13 - After class, the collected question papers are marked with credit (5 questions for 1+). They are returned after the exam.

Notice all the credit opportunities provided in this game: 1- the writing of questions, 2- the answering of questions, 3- the answering of missed questions by other team, 4- Just following the rules, by not calling out, all are ways students can earn credits.

CROSSWORD OR WORD SEARCH

Another type of game is the crossword or word-search. The information, words or definitions, are those that will be on the exam. As an example: suppose I make up a word-search puzzle. Copies are given out to the class. On the paper is the word-search puzzle, a list of words found in it and the credit rewards for doing the puzzle. Students are to circle the found words. The credit awards appear on the word search puzzle something as follows:

Words Found	Credits Earned
8-16	2
17-25	3
26-34	4
35-42	5
43-47	6
48-49	7
50	10

To mark the papers, have each student count up the number of words he has found and circle the number of credits earned. For example: a student has found 41 words, he should circle 5 in the credits earned column. **Students are permitted to work together, but they receive only half credit.**

Games are extremely useful in developing positive classroom attitudes. This is especially true if they are used to help the student review the classwork while at the same time earning credits.

* * * * *

THE MAJOR EXAMINATION

All major exams are worth 100%, except Mid-Terms and Finals which have a value of 200%. **Students may raise their grades one point for 5+ for regular exams, and one point for 10+ for Mid-Terms and the Final.** See previous chapter on how test marks may be eliminated. Mid-Term and Final grades may not be eliminated.

Now I'd like to write about the taking of the test. As long as tests have been in existence so has cheating. **Cheating is a chronic "poor work habit"** which exists on all levels of education. The Credit System enables the students to go into an exam with the security of knowing that if they do not do well, they can use the credits they earned to raise their test marks, or eliminate very poor ones altogether. This security will help to fight cheating on exams.

You're probably thinking that some students won't bother to study since they can get a good mark with their credits. This might happen but it cannot happen too often because no student will earn enough credit, through the term, to help him if he consistently gets poor grades.

Despite the above-mentioned security that credits give, students may still try to cheat. The technique I use to stop cheating cold is as follows:

1 - Give a "warning" to the student that you suspect him of trying to cheat or of not following some rule of taking a test.

2 - If this student persists in disobeying I give him a **HOLD** on his mark. A hold means that the student will never be able to raise or eliminate the mark on that particular exam, now or in the future, no matter how many credits he has accumulated. Usually, the "hold" penalty is explained to the class before the first major exam. At some point, you should write "HOLD" on the student's test paper. In my marking book, I will write the mark on this test with an "H." For example, a 75% mark would

be recorded as "75H," showing me that there is a "hold" on this mark.

I should point out that removing the student's ability to raise or eliminate test grades is not as severe as lowering his test mark, but it is severe enough. Just knowing the punishment will stop chronic cheaters because they have worked hard for their credits before the exam, and to lose the right to use them would be a very severe punishment in the context of the Credit System.

Besides the HOLD technique, credits, of course, may be earned during an exam, for neatness in writing (essays) and by answering unlimited-type questions as described in previous chapters.

CHAPTER X:
MONITORS & GOOD WORK HABITS

The use of monitors is often necessary to carry out certain tasks inside and/or outside the classroom. At the beginning of the term, a teacher knows very little about his students and may, without knowing it, chose a very untrustworthy student to do a job. However, by giving credit for a job <u>well done</u>, the teacher should get dependable service from any student. If a monitor fails to do a job to your satisfaction, you can use the technique of "denying credit." Since most students are eager to earn credits, they will do their best at the assigned job. <u>Monitorial service is a good way to provide credit opportunities to the non-academically inclined student.</u>

While many monitorial jobs are a "one-shot deal," some jobs can be assigned on a regular basis. For example, I like to have one student come in, before school begins, to work in my room in order to help straighten the room up, wash chalk boards, put up bulletin boards, etc. It is a convenience to have one student do this for a month or two. Therefore, this kind of monitor is given credits on a <u>salary basis</u>, perhaps 5+ a week or whatever you wish.

Here is a list of some types of monitors you may "employ" with a suggested credit award for the job:

1 - **Paper Distribution:** since you collect written work many times during the term, you will find it helpful to hire a few monitors to give out papers at the beginning of a class. Hire two to four students at 1+ each.

2 - **Clean Up:** A student or students are selected, at the beginning of a period, to go around the room with a waste paper basket to pick up papers. (3+ for this job)

3 - **Out of Room:** Sometimes a monitor is needed to go out of the room to get or bring things to the school office or some other place outside the classroom. Give 2+ if student returns in a reasonable time.

4 - **Carrying Equipment:** Books or school materials (give 3+)

5 - **Chalkboard:** Choose one student to erase the chalkboard "automatically" when he comes into the room. The job lasts one week and the student gets 1+ per day. (Salary basis)

I mentioned only a few monitorial jobs that you can give students. You can be sure that by using the Credit System these jobs will be done to the best of the student's ability.

Good Work Habits

One job that teachers find frustrating is getting a class seated and ready to work at the beginning of class. Students often come into a room yelling, running, hitting each other, going over to the window, etc. Here's how you handle this common occurrence using the Credit System.

IGNORE ALL STUDENTS EXCEPT THOSE IN THEIR SEATS DOING THE RIGHT THING. Start giving credits to those students. When the others see what is happening they will go to their seats also hoping to get a credit. The next time the class meets more students will get the idea. Some teachers in my school could not believe the ease with which I was able to get my classes ready to work. Many times I would explain the Credit System to these teachers and they would begin using it in their classes as well.

Here are some other "good work habits" you can give students credit for:

1 - having notebooks out copying the title (aim) of the lesson

2 - having a pen and pencil – conduct a "pen and pencil check" by having students hold up these items (1+)

3 - having textbook (if required by teacher that day)

4 - writing neatly

5 - having work in on time

6- in elementary school classes, group activities are common. Students can be given credits for cooperation, after the activity is over. The activity will run smoothly if the teacher reminds the children, occasionally, that "credits will be awarded after the activity is over."

Yes, there are many more examples. It is up to you to recognize them when they occur and give out credits to those students when appropriate.

* * * * *

In this section, I have described some of the typical types of classroom activities which lend themselves to the Credit System and how the System is employed as a motivational force to influence the development and continuance of positive student behavior. These activities are only suggestions and examples of what goes on in one particular classroom. The Credit System is so flexible it is adaptable to all classroom situations at any grade level.

I'm sure some of you will ask, "Am I going to be able to carry out the Credit System if I try it?" Believe me, when I say that when you see the positive response of your class or classes to the System you will want to carry it out. You will start making it a habit to continually look for positive acts by the students in order to reward them with credits. You will think of more and more rewards to offer the students to make their credits more valuable.

Why? Because your discipline problems will be cut to a minimum or even eliminated altogether.

You may ask, "Will students really want credits that much?" The answer is yes. As students earn credits they know that credits really do work to help them. This builds a sense of security and positive attitude towards your class, and hopefully school as well. They will gain self-esteem and have the satisfaction of knowing their everyday efforts are being recognized by the teacher and not forgotten. They will be encouraged to become responsible in their work and monitorial jobs.

Security, confidence, self-esteem and responsibility are all produced in a Credit System classroom.

Another question some of you may have is, “Won’t students care only about earning credits and not about learning the subject matter?” If we remember, when we went to school, we didn’t like or care about all our subjects either. The Credit System is an incentive for the students to give you a chance to present the subject matter in the best possible way that you can.

Remember: THE CREDIT SYSTEM IS A SUPPLEMENT TO AND NOT A REPLACEMENT FOR THE SUBJECT MATTER TAUGHT IN YOUR CLASS.

SECTION 4

CREDITS vs POOR WORK HABITS AND DISCIPLINE PROBLEMS

CHAPTER XI:
CREDITS VS. POOR WORK HABITS

The Credit System was invented in response to student poor work and discipline problems in my classroom. These problems are the reasons why capable teachers fail to teach and capable students fail to learn. In the college education courses that I took, very little was taught, if anything, about controlling a class. Yet without discipline, all the teacher's knowledge will mean nothing. Millions of hours are wasted and lost because of behavior problems. Eliminate these problems and American education will become many times more productive then it is now.

In this chapter, I'm going to discuss techniques, used to eliminate poor work habits. Poor work habits often develop without the teacher realizing it. In a sense, they are harder to correct since they do not easily lend themselves to traditional discipline techniques. However, using the Credit System makes them easier to control.

* * * * *

One of the axioms of the Credit System is that <u>students would rather use than lose their credits</u>. Therefore, students will try to avoid credit loss, if possible. In previous chapters, I have discussed just such possible losses. Briefly, here is a summary of such techniques:

1 - **Loss of Credit Opportunity:** denying credit to a student, where he ordinarily would be entitled to earn

credit, because of some poor work habit. Shouting out an answer, would be such a time.

2 - **Loss of Immediacy of Reward:** The postponement of a reward because of poor work habits or behavior (Probation). The student may get the reward at a later date if improvement is shown.

3 - **Loss of Credit Power:** Example: getting a "Hold" on a major exam, thereby losing the ability to raise or eliminate test marks.

4 - **Involuntary Use of Credits:** Whereby students must "spend" their credits to "pay" for a poor work habit, such as not handing a piece of written work on time.

All of the ways of controlling poor work habits and poor student behavior are variations of the above techniques. Experienced teachers have come to know what to expect from students. It is a question of being <u>prepared</u> to deal with the problems and not be taken by surprise each time. Using the Credit System helps submerge or at least delay these problems, and it will not let troublemakers spread their mischief to the entire class.

Remember, the traditional discipline techniques, i.e. letters home, calling up parents, parent-teacher conferences, sending students to the dean, etc. are still available if needed.

In this chapter, I will discuss the elimination of poor work habits using the Credit System. Poor work habits, if not controlled early on, will eventually lead to more serious behavior problems.

An example of a common poor work habit is excessive leaving the class "to go to the bathroom." It is difficult to say no to a student who has "to go" because it just might be the "emergency" he says it is. So here's how you handle this problem. Tell the class, at the beginning of the year, that every student will be permitted to leave the room **five FREE times** during the year. (Record date of FREE time out on card in order to keep track of number of times student left class) After the fifth time the student must **"pay"** 10+ if he wants to leave (Involuntary use of credit). This method gives the student plenty of times to go to the bathroom without loss of credit and therefore he is more likely to leave your room when he really has to. Any FREE times left, at the end of the year, will be traded in for 5+. You may ask, "Will this really work ?" I've used this method right from the inception of the Credit System, so believe me when I tell you it does.

Let's continue with some more poor work habits, that haven't been discussed previously, and the Credit System techniques for reducing and eliminating them.

LATENESS TO CLASS - Tell the ·students that any student coming late to class, without a late pass, will be charged one of his "free times out" of the room. If he has no free times left, he will have to pay 10+.

LEAVING CLASS BEFORE SIGNAL - If a student leaves before the signal is given, that student is considered to be out of the room and is charged one free time out, or 10+ if he has no free time outs left.

NOT BEING READY TO WORK - Give credits to students who are seated AND are prepared to work. They have pen and /or pencil, and open notebook on desk. They are copying "aim of lesson" and any homework assignments.

NOT GETTING SEATED - Give credits to all seated students who are ready, while ignoring all others.

NOT HAVING A PENCIL, PEN OR NOTEBOOK - Once in a while, have a "pen check." Have students hold up their pens. Give 1+ to prepared students. Any student who has no writing instrument must "rent" a pencil for 10+. (Keep a supply of pencils available.) At end of period, when student returns the pencil, he gets back 5+. He may keep the pencil at the cost of 10+. (Purchasing material objects can be considered another reward of the System.)

* * * * *

Besides the poor work habits, mentioned above, I have discussed in previous chapters how to use the Credit System to control other poor work habits, such as sloppy written work , improper behavior by monitors, handing in written work on time, calling out during class discussion, etc.

It is not my intention to mention every poor work habit that is possible. My intention is to get the teacher to start thinking in certain ways in order to eliminate these poor work habits that, if not controlled, can lead to disruptive behavior which will destroy a class. In the next chapter, I intend to discuss how the Credit System helps me to deal with these serious problems.

CHAPTER XII : CONTROLLING POOR BEHAVIOR

In a previous chapter, I wrote that the Credit System is not a substitute for the subject matter. What the Credit System enables a teacher to do is teach the best way he or she can. If you make the subject matter as interesting and meaningful as possible, the majority of students will want to learn.

Nevertheless there are students who will not respond to subject matter. Many of these students will respond to the rewards of the Credit System. This leaves us with a very small number of students who may respond to neither. These students will earn credits for awhile but then they may start to "act up." You will find that these students will "isolate" themselves, since the vast majority of students in your classes will have experienced success and will not wish to spoil their records. The fact is most students do want to learn when they come to school. Most of them resent it when other students try disruptive behavior and get away with it.

In this chapter, I'm going to discuss some techniques that I use to control poor behavior problems that develop in the classroom.

OFFICIAL WARNINGS

This is a warning to an offending student, telling him that if he continues to violate the rules of conduct of the class he will be **FINED. A "fine"** is the removal of one or more credits from the student's credit balance to "pay" for some act of misbehavior.

At an appropriate time, I usually spend a few minutes explaining warnings and fines. I tell them that an **"Official Warning"** is a courtesy extended to the student to let him know that he is violating class procedures. If the student continues this behavior "from this point on to the end of the period" he will have 1+ removed from his card for each offense. I point out that this poor behavior not only hurts himself, but will deprive the class of learning time, which will lessen the opportunity of other students to learn and earn credits . <u>By saying this you will put group pressure on the misbehaving student. Since the vast majority of the class wants to be able to earn as many credits as possible during class.</u>

You have now set up a way of dealing with misbehavior. The "act of misbehavior" will be punished. Discipline will be fair and impersonal (the student's character won't be attacked – which only breeds resentment). Every student knows where he stands; there will be no favoritism or scapegoats. If the offending student stops his misbehavior, there is NO loss of credits whatsoever.

Remember, the class has been building up their credits through some form of effort (oral, written, monitorial through the previous weeks of the term. Students just do not want to lose their hard-earned credits, therefore they find no "heroism" in the acts of the troublemakers. They will not join the disruptive student and he will find himself alone in his attempts to create class chaos.

Thwarted in this, he may settle down again and continue to learn and earn credit as before. If not, you still have the Dean's Office, and other traditional punishments for disruptive students.

FINES

The first "fining situation" also involves some strategy. Fining of even 1+ is very serious business. The teacher should not use fines unless absolutely necessary. However, if it comes down to it, show that you don't enjoy removing credits from any student's card. For example, you might say, "I know you have been a good student and you are a fine person, but you were given an Official Warning and so I must remove one credit for your continued behavior. I'm sorry about this but I'm sure before the period is over you will earn back the credit you have just lost."

You see how easily you are able to separate poor student behavior from the student himself. The punishment is fair and will be supported by the class. Most important, you will not have alienated the student, which would have damaged your relationship. Students know when they are doing the wrong thing and if the punishment is fair they will accept it and respect you as well.

SUSPENSION OF CREDIT

After the first fine, if a student continues to misbehave, I make it a rule that he is permitted two more fines, for a total of 3+ off his credit balance. After the third fine, I will inform the student that if he gets fined one more time he will receive a SUSPENSION OF CREDIT. This means that a student may continue to earn credits as before but that he may not use any of them for any reason. I will write an "S" on his card to remind me that the student is "under suspension."

Suspensions of Credit must be removed before a student can use any his credits and that goes for the Conduct Tax. (Therefore, the student may not get an "A" in conduct if he has a Suspension, even though he may have enough credits to "pay" for a good conduct mark). Here are some suggested ways Suspensions of Credit may be removed by the student:

1 - **A Letter of Apology:** for the first time offender a simple "I'm sorry for (the offense) and I promise not to do it again," will suffice. The student signs and dates the letter and hands it to you. Remove the "S" from his card and file the letter. (All written notes should be filed).

2 - **A Letter of Apology signed by student and parent.** (2nd time)

3 - **A Written Assignment on Behavior in Class.** For example, "Why listening in class is important," or something similar. Make it 50 or more words, to be signed by both child and parent. (3rd time)

4 - **Removal of Credits** (25+) if student refuses to remove Suspension on his own within two school days or if a student misbehaves while under suspension, the 25+ is removed immediately, the suspension removed and a 1+ fine is given.

If the student still persists in disruptive behavior, then traditional techniques such as a parent conference, calling the Dean, removal from class, etc., may be in order. In any case, this student will NOT succeed in getting the other students to start causing trouble thanks to the power of the Credit System.

CREDIT TRANSFERS

This technique simply means that credits are transferred from one student's card to another. This may be done either voluntarily or involuntarily. For example, if one student is bothering another, you can threaten to "transfer credit" if the offending student continues.

LOW CREDIT BALANCE TECHNIQUES

What happens if an offending student has too few credits to "pay" for his misdeeds? Here is what you do:

1 - If a student is fined more credits than he has, you "lend" him credits to pay the fine. (Loaned credits are written as "minuses" (-).

2 - As he earns credit, the minuses are crossed off.

3 - You can" lend" him up to five minuses after which he can do two things: a) you can deduct 1+ from a major exam (this eliminates the five minuses), or b) have another student lend him five credits (Voluntary credit transfer)

Now that I have discussed the techniques, in the next chapter I will give you specific poor behavior problems and my suggestions on how to handle them.

CHAPTER XIII: CREDITS vs. POOR BEHAVIOR

Now that you are "armed" with the techniques described in the previous chapter, you are prepared to deal with some common discipline problems. In this chapter, I will list these problems and suggest ways of handling them.

ANNOYING OTHER STUDENTS - Let's say Student A is annoying Student B. By this I mean that B wants nothing to do with A. There are several possibilities here. You could:

1 - change A's or B's seat and charge A 5+ for the **"service."**

2 - give official warning to A

3 - threaten Credit Transfer from A to B

CALLING OUT - If the calling out is in response to a question simply "deny credit," otherwise give offending student an "Official Warning."

CURSING - An automatic 5+ fine on the first occurrence with a Suspension of Credit. Have student write essay on "Why Bad Language is Inappropriate in the Classroom."

CUTTING - The Credit System tends to encourage attendance since most students, including cutters, like the System. You might work out a private agreement to pay the student 1+ for attending class.

FALLING OFF CHAIRS - Watch for a student who tilts his chair and tell him to keep the chair straight. If he does fall, first see if he's hurt, then give him a Suspension of Credit. Have him write an essay on the "Proper Way of Sitting on a Chair."

You might announce that "any student falling off a chair will receive an automatic fine."

FIGHTING - If a fight breaks out, "hire" three or four monitors to keep other students away from the fighters. Go over to the fighters and say loudly, "I am going to start counting, for each number I count, 2+ will be deducted from your cards. I will stop counting as soon as you break apart. Ready?" Saying all these things acts as a warning and in most cases the fighting will stop. If it doesn't stop by the count of five, have the hired monitors break up the fight.

After the class, hold a conference with the fighters. Tell them they both have a Suspension of Credit. In order to remove it, both students must hand in a written explanation for the fight.

FOOLING AROUND WITH MATERIALS - At the end of a period, or while leaving the room, some students like to touch and play with available materials or write on the chalkboard when you're not looking. Simply say there is a 25+ charge for doing these things and that should solve the problem.

GUM CHEWING - Tell them that gum chewing is permitted in your class with the following rules:

1 - the gum chewer must inform you first.

2 - it will cost the student 15+

3 - gum must be chewed quietly (no popping or cracking)

4 - gum must be disposed of in a gum wrapper, in the waste basket at the end of the period.

5 - not following these rules will result in an automatic fine (20+) and a banning of any further gum chewing for the remainder of the marking period.(Put "G" on card)

6 - Of course, the above is optional. If you find gum chewing objectionable, forbid it altogether.

INATTENTION - Use traditional methods, such as calling on a student to answer a question. If the student doesn't know the question, charge him 1+ for having to repeat the question. Tell him you had to work "overtime" and therefore the student has to pay for the extra time.

OUT OF SEAT WITHOUT PERMISSION - There is no good reason for students to be out of their seats without permission. Usually, a student gets out of his seat to "throw away a piece of paper" in order to gain attention or talk to a friend not seated near him. If there is some real reason for the student to get out of his seat, he must first ask permission by raising his hand. If a student does get up, stop the class, tell him to get seated immediately or else he will be "Fined." On a second offense, give the student a "Suspension of Credit" and tell him to write a short essay on the "Proper Way of Leaving My Seat During Class." Remove the Suspension when this is handed in and file the essay.

RUDENESS - If a student is rude to another student or to you, get an immediate apology. Threaten the student with a Fine or Suspension of Credit if it happens again. Transfer of credit is another option.

SITTING IN IMPROPER SEAT - When a student knowingly sits in a seat not assigned to him, he is challenging your authority. I advise you to first tell the student that he is "not in his assigned seat" and tell him to move. If he refuses then it is time to use the Credit System. Tell him that you are going to write down the time. For every 1 minute he is in the wrong seat he will lose 10+. (I call this a RATE FINE, in this case the rate is 10+/minute) Since most students do not want to lose their hard-earned credit, they will usually move in a few seconds.

SPITTING - automatic 10+ Fine and Suspension. Have him write essay on "Why You Shouldn't Spit in Class."

STEALING - If the student is known, have student return property as soon as possible. Suspend credit and have student write a report about why it important to be honest. If the student is not known, and you feel some-one in the class knows who did it, tell the class that all students' credits are suspended until the thief comes forward. This puts tremendous peer pressure on the guilty party.

THROWING OBJECTS - If the student is known, give him an automatic 10+ Fine and Suspension. To take off the Suspension he must come in the next morning or stay late to clean up the floor. If he refuses, he will pay 10+ for a monitor to do the job and an additional 25+ to have his Suspension taken off. If the student is not known, use same technique as in stealing; announce all students in class will have their credits suspended until guilty student comes forward.

WHISPERING OR TALKING - Use same technique as for Inattentive student (see INATTENTION). Warnings, Fines and Suspension of Credit to follow if talker persists.

WRITING ON DESKS - The first time you spot a student doing this, speak to him privately about the matter. See if you can get the student to clean up the mess voluntarily after class. (Always keep a supply of steel wool pads, a sponge, towels, and a water basin for just such times). Tell him if he cannot or won't do it, you will "hire" a monitor who will be paid 15+ by the offending student (Credit Transfer).

* * * * *

Discipline problems are like pain. We don't like it but it is a warning that something is wrong. The techniques described in the chapter are effective for a while, but the teacher should look further to find out why these problems are coming about. Often, the student himself is incapable of any kind of self-control and is in need of outside help, Whatever the cause, the teacher should work on a student who has a chronic problem. A possible suggestion is to have a private plan (such as in the case of the cutter) whereby credits may be earned for the student's cooperation.

In this chapter, I have discussed many types of discipline problems that may occur in the classroom. Using the Credit System you will be able to keep them to a minimum, and most important, the problem will not become class wide. For the most part, these techniques are in-the-class solutions, that is, they do not require help from parents, deans or guidance counselors, social workers, psychologists, etc. However, all these people are still available and should be used if all else falls.

CHAPTER XIV: SOME FINAL THOUGHTS

What is the Credit System? The Credit System is a form of "behavior modification" called a token economy. In a token economy, immediate rewards (in this case the credit) can be traded in for deferred rewards (all the other rewards offered in the Credit System).

I have to tell you that I found out about token systems after I was using it for a few years. I read as much literature as I could about token systems, but none of them was quite the same or as easy to put into action as the Credit System. The main problem with token systems is the bookkeeping, but the Credit System is so easy to institute that the problem is easily overcome.

Another advantage is the deferred rewards have to be requested by the student. The teacher doesn't have to keep careful records of what and when rewards have to be given. The easier the System is to begin and continue, the more likely that it will be continued indefinitely.

The System works for many reasons. Here are a few of them:

1 - the Credit is controlled by the student. They don't have to use them for anything, with the exception of the conduct tax.

2 - the System is tied into the school system by the conduct tax. This gives the students an immediate reason to want to earn credits.

3 - Credits are “earned” not given at the whim of a teacher. A tiny drop of sweat is in each credit. Students will think carefully before using them.

4 - The loss of even one credit, through fining or for some poor work habit, seems even greater than it really is, since the student doesn’t know exactly how much he has at any one time. Therefore, the effect of fining will be magnified and far more effective than giving meaningless “zeroes.”

5 - The Credit System is positive, and will be viewed as such by the class. Since the class will exhibit positive behavior, so will the teacher and so the System becomes self-perpetuating.

6 - There are no actual materials transferred from teacher to student. There is nothing that a student can lose. Credits are actually just numbers which have no physical reality, but have real power.

7 - The deferred rewards are meaningful for improving student behavior and work. They are rewards that could not be bought in a store, but can be “purchased” only through the student’s good work and acts.

I suppose I could go on and on but, just like a book on How to Play Golf, the only way to convince you of the power and effectiveness of the Credit System is for you to try it. When you do, I know you will enjoy teaching and your class will enjoy learning.

The beauty of the System is that it is limited only to the imagination of the teacher. The ideas in this book are merely suggestions. You can use them or not, but one thing I can assure you, the Credit System will work! Best of luck.

GLOSSARY OF TERMS

CONDUCT TAX - the number of credits (35+ – 50+) needed by student to get an "A" in conduct. These credits may not be used during a marking period and are removed only at the end of a marking period. P. 14

CREDIT - The basic unit of the Credit System. It symbolizes one act of positive student behavior. Symbol: 1+ P. 12-13

CREDIT AWARDS - The number of credits given for doing something such as homework , games, etc.

CREDIT BALANCE - the number of credits the student has accumulated during the term. The credit balance is recorded on a seating plan book card or chart. P. 23

CREDIT BOND (40+) - a certificate which the student buys with credit. After a certain amount of time it is redeemed for 50+. P.32

CREDIT CHARGE - the "cost" of a reward.

CREDIT COUNT - informing the students of his credit balance. P. 23

CREDIT OPPORTUNITIES - written, oral or monitorial chances for the student to earn credits.

CREDIT SYSTEM - the system of immediate and deferred rewards used to encourage students to exhibit and continue positive classroom behavior.

CREDITS, LOANED - credits loaned by the teacher (up to 5+) to help student, who has no credits, to "pay" a fine. P. 72

CREDITS, USABLE - credits which may be used by the students for various credit rewards.

DENYING CREDIT - the technique of not giving credit for a positive student act because of a poor work habit., i.e. calling out a correct answer during class discussion. P. 63

ELIMINATION OF MARKS - using credits to eliminate test and report marks from a student's average.

FINE - removal of cr edit from a student's credit balance in order to pay for a discipline problem. P. 70

FREE TIMES OUT - the number of times a student may leave the room (usually five) before he has to "pay" for the privilege. P. 65

HOLD - the penalty whereby the student loses his ability to use his credits to raise or eliminate the mark on that particular major exam. Put an "H" on test paper. P. 54

INSTANT REPORT CARD (5+) - the student's ability to find out the exact work mark he would get on his report card at that moment. P. 32

PLUS (+) SIGN - the symbol for the credit, i.e. 1+ stands for one credit, 3+ stands for three credits, etc.

PROBATION - a stated period of time (such as one week) a student must wait to get a reward. Usually, the wait is imposed because of some student discipline problem. P. 26

REQUEST SHEET - a sheet a student hands in to request a reward. It must be headed (name and class) with the type of reward wanted. P. 25

REWARD, DEFERRED - rewards obtained by trading in credits. P.79

REWARD, IMMEDIATE - the credit. Given immediately after some type of positive behavior or work. P. 79

SEATING PLAN BOOK - the most useful way of keeping track of students and their credits. These books are published by the Delaney Co. and Arco. They are obtainable through teacher supply houses or college book stores. If you cannot get one, use a seating plan chart that has plenty of room. P. 12, 20

SEATING PLAN CARD - cards used with seating plan book . Individual student's credits are recorded on these. P. 12, 20

SPECIAL COUNT (1+) - if student wants to know his credit balance immediately he can ask you for a special count. For 1+ count up his credits. P. 24

SUSPENSION - the condition under which a student cannot use his credits for any deferred rewards. He may earn credits as normal. P. 70-71

SUSPENSION REQUIREMENT - the requirement set up by the teacher for the student to remove his suspension. P. 70-71

TRANSFER OF CREDIT - the technique of exchanging a certain number of credits from one student to another. P. 72

WARNING - warning given to student that he is in danger of being "fined." P. 69

WORK, UNLIMITED - Work which has no definite ending, such as the making a lists in a certain amount of

time. These types of work are marked on a "rate basis," such as: for every five items the student earns 1+.
P. 42-43.

BOARD OF EDUCATION OF THE CITY OF NEW YORK

BUREAU OF EDUCATIONAL AND VOCATIONAL GUIDANCE

SUPERVISOR OF GUIDANCE
SCHOOL DISTRICT 22

TELEPHONE: [illegible]

ALBERT SCHWARTZ
PUBLIC SCHOOL [illegible]
[illegible] AVENUE
BROOKLYN, N. Y. [illegible]

January 14, 1974

Mr. Arthur Kaplan
J. H. S. 78
1420 East 68th Street
Brooklyn, New York 11234

Dear Mr. Kaplan:

As per my promise to you, I am writing to invite you to be a participant in the Behavior Modification Mini-Course I have arranged for the Guidance Counselors of this District. The course will meet for four sessions on Wednesday afternoons, February 6, 13, 20 and 27 in Room 111 of the District Office. Sessions will run from 3:30 to 5:10 P.M. and will be conducted under the direction of Mr. Gene Cash of the Flatlands Guidance Center.

Please drop me a note at your earliest convenience to let me know whether or not you plan to participate. You are, incidentally, the only non-guidance counselor who has been invited to enroll.

Cordially,

Albert Schwartz

ALBERT SCHWARTZ

AS:nf

CC: Mr. Edwin Katz, Principal
J.H.S. 78

BOARD OF EDUCATION OF THE CITY OF NEW YORK

BUREAU OF EDUCATIONAL AND VOCATIONAL GUIDANCE

SUPERVISOR OF GUIDANCE
SCHOOL DISTRICT 22

ALBERT SCHWARTZ
PUBLIC SCHOOL [illegible]
[illegible] AVENUE
BROOKLYN, N. Y. [illegible]

TELEPHONE [illegible]

February 26, 1974

Mr. Arthur Kaplan
I. S. 78
1420 East 68th Street
Brooklyn, New York 11234

Dear Mr. Kaplan:

This is to let you know how much I appreciate your outstanding contributions to the Behavior Modification Seminars. The counselors who have been participating have been impressed with your enthusiasm and the variety of techniques you have discussed. I trust that you, too, have found the sessions fruitful and adaptable to your work in the classroom. I should, of course, appreciate any feedback you would care to offer.

You may also wish to recall my original suggestion to you that you consider the possibility of preparing some of your material for publication. Should you wish to do so, I would be pleased to help.

Again, please accept my sincere congratulations for your excellent contributions to the Behavior Modification Seminars.

Cordially,

Albert Schwartz

ALBERT SCHWARTZ
Supervisor of Guidance

AS:mf

cc: Mr. Edwin Katz
Principal, I. S. 78

BOARD OF EDUCATION OF THE CITY OF NEW YORK

BUREAU OF EDUCATIONAL AND VOCATIONAL GUIDANCE

SUPERVISOR OF GUIDANCE
SCHOOL DISTRICT 22

ALBERT SCHWARTZ
PUBLIC SCHOOL [illegible]
[illegible] AVENUE
BROOKLYN, N. Y. [illegible]

TELEPHONE [illegible]

March 15, 1974

Mr. Arthur Kaplan
J.H.S. 78
1420 East 68th Street
Brooklyn, New York 11234

Dear Mr. Kaplan:

I am enclosing your Certificate of Completion for the Behavior Modification Mini-Course with my repeated thanks for your contributions there. I have also received your letter requesting my reactions to your idea regarding the preparation of a pamphlet delineating your application of Behavior Modification techniques in the classroom. As I suggested to you earlier during one of our conferences, I think that it would be an excellent idea and might even have commercial possibilities. I feel that the specific techniques that you have developed represent practical and realistic applications of Behavior Modification theories and that these applications could profitably be utilized by teachers in a variety of classroom situations. As I offered earlier, I would be happy to discuss the project with you at greater length at a mutually convenient time.

Whatever you decide to do, please accept my thanks and best wishes for continued success.

Cordially,

Albert Schwartz

ALBERT SCHWARTZ
Supervisor of Guidance

AS:mf

Enc.

ACKNOWLEDGMENTS

I would like to acknowledge some of the people who influenced me, directly or indirectly, in the creation of the idea of the Credit System and the book itself.

First to my late wife. Eileen, who through almost 49 years of marriage gave me so much love, happiness and support.

To my son Jeff and my daughter-in-law, Anna who give me love and support everyday.

To my brother, Jack, who I have known and loved my entire life, for helping with graphics and "look" of this book. Along with other numerous suggestions to make the book "flow" for the reader.

To my former colleagues, Mel Berger and Carol Radil-off, teachers at my school Roy H. Mann in Brooklyn, with whom I shared my ideas . We spent many hours talking about new ways the Credit System could be used to help the teacher and the student achieve suc-cess.

To Albert Schwartz, Supervisor of Guidance in District 22K, who gave me a chance to speak to the guidance counselors of the District, about my ideas of controlling student discipline problems, and who encouraged me to write down these ideas for publication.

To the many teachers who introduced the System into their classroom and wrote to me of how the System affected their teaching experience and the attitudes of their students.

Speaking of which, I'd also like to acknowledge a former student of mine Butch Iacaobelli. Butch was an average student in my class who requested one of the rewards of the Credit System. Afterwards he greatly improved his classroom performance. Years later he told me that the reward "changed his life." Today he is a captain of a fishing boat in Costa Rica taking tourists out for a day of fishing in the Pacific. To this day we still communicate with each other. He has never forgotten me and I have not forgotten him.

Art Kaplan